THE DOCK

A Play

by

JOHN MORTIMER

SAMUEL FRENCH

LONDON
NEW YORK TORONTO SYDNEY HOLLYWOOD

ISBN 0 573 04209 8

CHARACTERS

MORGENHALL, an unsuccessful barrister
FOWLE, an unsuccessful criminal

*The action of the Play is in two Scenes and passes in a
prison cell*

Time—the present

THE DOCK BRIEF

SCENE I

SCENE—*A prison cell.*
The walls are grey and fade upwards into the shadows, so that the ceiling is not seen, and it might even be possible to escape upwards. The door, up one step, is L of the back wall, and there is a small barred window high up in the wall R, through which the sky looks very blue. There is a bed, with a pillow and two dark blankets, against the wall L. A small table stands R of the door, with a Bible on it, and an enamel bucket under it. R of the window is a towel-rail with a towel. Under the window there is a chair with a stool on top of it.
(See the Ground Plan at the end of the Play)

When the CURTAIN *rises,* FOWLE, *a small, fat man, is standing on the stool on tip-toe, his hands in his pockets. He is peering out of the window at the sky. The bolts of the door shoot back and the door opens.* MORGENHALL *strides in. He is an aged barrister with appearance of a dusty vulture, dressed in a black gown and bands. He carries a brief-case and his legal wig. He stands by the door and speaks to an unseen warder off.*

MORGENHALL. Is this where—you keep Mr Fowle? Good, excellent. (*He turns to the table, puts down his brief-case and wig, moves* C *and looks towards the door,* Then leave us alone like a good fellow. Would you mind closing the door? These old places are so draughty.

(*The door closes. The bolts shoot back*)

(*He looks around*) Mr Fowle—where are you, Mr

Fowle? Not escaped, I pray. (*He looks around and sees Fowle*) Good Heavens, man, come down. Come down, Mr Fowle.

    (MORGENHALL *darts at Fowle and there is a struggle he pulls the bewildered* FOWLE *down*)

I haven't hurt you? (*He takes the stool from the chair and sets it on the floor* LC)

    (FOWLE *makes a negative-sounding noise*)

I was suddenly anxious. A man in your unfortunate position. Desperate measures. And I couldn't bear to lose you. No, don't stand up. It's difficult for you without braces, or a belt, I can see. And no tie, no shoelaces. I'm so glad they're looking after you. You must forgive me if I frightened you just a little, Mr Fowle. It was when I saw you up by that window . . .

  FOWLE (*in a hoarse and sad voice*) Epping Forest.

  MORGENHALL (*turning to him*) What did you say?

  FOWLE. I think you can see Epping Forest.

  MORGENHALL. No doubt you can. But why, my dear chap, why should you want to?

  FOWLE. It's the home stretch.

  MORGENHALL. Very well.

  FOWLE. I thought I could get a glimpse of the green. Between the chimneys and that shed . . . (*He climbs on to the chair*)

    (MORGENHALL *crosses to* FOWLE *and there is a brief renewed struggle*)

  MORGENHALL. No, get down. It's not wise to be up there, forever trying to look out. There's a draughty, sneeping wind. Treacherous. (*He draws Fowle* c)

  FOWLE. Treacherous?

  MORGENHALL. I'm afraid so. You never know what a mean, sneeping wind can do. Catch you by the throat, start a sneeze, then a dry tickle on the chest, I don't want anything to catch you like that before . . .

  FOWLE. Before what?

  MORGENHALL. You're much better sitting quietly down here in the warm.

(FOWLE *crosses and sits on the bed*)
Just sit quietly and I'll introduce myself. (*He takes off
his gown and puts it on the upstage end of the bed*)
FOWLE. I am tired.
MORGENHALL. I'm Morgenhall. (*He sits on the stool*)
FOWLE. Morgenhall?
MORGENHALL. Morgenhall. The barrister.
FOWLE. The barrister?
MORGENHALL. Perfectly so.
FOWLE. I'm sorry.
MORGENHALL. Why?
FOWLE. A barrister. That's very bad.
MORGENHALL. I don't know. Why's it so bad?
FOWLE. When a gentleman of your stamp goes
wrong. A long fall.
MORGENHALL. What can you mean?
FOWLE. Different for an individual like me. I only
kept a small seed shop.
MORGENHALL. Seed shop? My poor fellow. We
mustn't let this unfortunate little case confuse us.
We're going to come to important decisions. Now, do
me a favour, Mr Fowle, no more seed shops.
FOWLE. Bird-seed, of course. Individuals down our
way kept birds mostly. Canaries and budgies. The
budgies talked. Lot of lonely people down our way.
They kept them for the talk.
MORGENHALL. Mr Fowle. I'm a barrister.
FOWLE. Tragic.
MORGENHALL. I know the law.
FOWLE. It's trapped you.
MORGENHALL. I'm here to help you.
FOWLE. We'll help each other.

(*There is a pause then* MORGENHALL *laughs un-
controllably*)

MORGENHALL. I see. Mr Fowle, I see where you've
been bewildered. You think I'm in trouble as well.
Then I've got good news for you at last. I'm free. Oh,
yes, I can leave here when I like.
FOWLE. Can you?
MORGENHALL. The police are my friends.

FOWLE. They are?

MORGENHALL. And I've never felt better in my life. There now. That's relieved you, hasn't it? I'm not in any trouble. (*He takes his spectacle case from his pocket and puts on his spectacles*)

FOWLE. Family all well?

MORGENHALL. I never married.

FOWLE. Rent paid up?

MORGENHALL. A week or two owing, perhaps. Temporary lull in business. This case will end all that.

FOWLE. Which case?

MORGENHALL. Your case.

FOWLE. My . . . ?

MORGENHALL. Case.

FOWLE. Oh, that—it's not important.

MORGENHALL. Not?

FOWLE (*rising*) I don't care about it to any large extent. Not as at present advised.

MORGENHALL. Mr Fowle. How could you say that?

FOWLE. The flavour's gone out of it.

MORGENHALL. But we're only at the beginning.

FOWLE (*crossing to* C) I can't believe it's me concerned.

MORGENHALL. But it is you, Mr Fowle. You mustn't let yourself forget that. You see, that's why you're here.

FOWLE. I can't seem to bother with it. (*He moves up* C)

MORGENHALL. Can you be so busy?

FOWLE. Slopping in, slopping out. (*He moves down* RC) Peering at the old forest. It fills in the day.

MORGENHALL. You seem, if I may say so—(*he rises*) to have adopted an unpleasantly selfish attitude.

FOWLE. Selfish?

MORGENHALL. Dog in a manger. (*He moves* C)

FOWLE. In the . . . ?

MORGENHALL. Unenthusiastic.

FOWLE. You're speaking quite frankly, I well appreciate . . .

MORGENHALL. I'm sorry, Fowle. You made me say it. There's so much of this about, nowadays. There's so much ready-made entertainment. Free billiards,

National Health, Television. There's not the spirit
abroad there used to be.

FOWLE. You feel that?

MORGENHALL. Whatever I've done, I've always been
mustard keen on my work. I've never lost the vision,
Fowle. In all my disappointments I've never lost the
love of the job.

FOWLE. The position in life you've obtained to.

MORGENHALL. Years of study I had to put in. It
didn't just drop in my lap.

FOWLE. I've never studied. (*He sits on the chair* R)

MORGENHALL. Year after year, Fowle, my window at
college was alight until two a.m. There I sat among my
books. I fed mainly on herrings . . .

FOWLE. Lean years?

MORGENHALL. And black tea. No subsidized biscuits,
then, Fowle, no County Council tobacco, just work.

FOWLE. Bookwork, almost entirely? I'm only assum-
ing that, of course.

MORGENHALL. Want to hear some Latin?

FOWLE. Only if you have time.

MORGENHALL. *Actus non sit reus nisi mens sit rea.
Filius. Nullius In flagrante delicto.* Understand it?
(*He removes his spectacles*)

FOWLE. I'm no scholar.

MORGENHALL. You most certainly are not. But I had
to be, we all had to be in my day. Then we'd sit for
the examinations; mods, smalls, greats, tripos, little
goes—rowing men fainting, Indian students vomiting
with fear, and no creeping out for a peep at the book
under the pretext of a pump ship or getting a glance at
the other fellow's celluloid cuff.

FOWLE. That would be very unheard of?

MORGENHALL. Then weeks, months of waiting. (*He
crosses to* L) Nerve racking. Go up to the Lake District.
Pace the mountains, play draughts—(*he crosses to* C)
forget to huff. (*He moves up* RC) Then comes the fatal
postcard.

FOWLE. What's it say?

MORGENHALL. Satisfied the examiners.

FOWLE. Well done!

MORGENHALL. Don't rejoice so soon. True enough, I felt I'd turned a corner, got a fur hood, bumped on the head with a Bible. Told the only lady in my life that in five years' time, perhaps . . .

FOWLE. You'd arrived.

MORGENHALL. That's what I thought when they painted my name up on my London chambers. I sat down to fill in the time until they sent my first brief in a real case. I sat down to do the crossword puzzle while I waited. Five years later, Fowle, what was I doing?

FOWLE. A little charge of High Treason?

MORGENHALL. I was still doing the crossword puzzle.

FOWLE. But better at it?

MORGENHALL. Not much. Not very much. As the years pass there come to be clues you no longer understand.

FOWLE. So all that training?

MORGENHALL. Wasted. The talents rust.

FOWLE. And the lady?

MORGENHALL. Drove an ambulance, in the nineteen-fourteen. A stray piece of shrapnel took her. (*He picks up his brief-case*) I don't care to talk of it.

FOWLE. Tragic.

MORGENHALL. It was.

FOWLE. Tragic my wife was never called up.

MORGENHALL (*moving down* C) You mustn't talk like that, Fowle, your poor wife.

FOWLE. Don't let's carry on about me.

MORGENHALL. But we must carry on about you. That's what I'm here for.

FOWLE. You're here to . . .

MORGENHALL. To defend you. (*He crosses to* LC *and puts the brief-case on the stool*)

FOWLE. Can't be done.

MORGENHALL. Why ever not?

FOWLE. I know who killed her.

MORGENHALL. Who?

FOWLE. Me.

(*There is a pause.* MORGENHALL *swings round up* L, *and after considerable thought, giggles*)

MORGENHALL. Really, Mr Fowle, I have all the respect in the world for your opinions, but we must face this. You're a man of very little education.

FOWLE. That's true.

MORGENHALL. One has only to glance at you to see that you're a person of very limited intelligence. (*He crosses to Fowle*)

FOWLE. Agreed, quite frankly.

MORGENHALL. You think you killed your wife.

FOWLE. Seems so to me.

MORGENHALL. Mr Fowle. Look at yourself objectively. On questions of bird-seed I have no doubt you may be infallible—but on a vital point like this might you not be mistaken? Don't answer . . .

FOWLE. Why not, sir?

MORGENHALL. Before you drop the bomb of a reply, consider who will be wounded. Are the innocent to suffer?

FOWLE. I only want to be honest.

MORGENHALL. But you're a criminal, Mr Fowle. You've broken through the narrow fabric of honesty. You are free to be kind, human, to do good.

FOWLE. But what I did to her . . .

MORGENHALL. She's passed, you know, out of your life. You've set up new relationships. You've picked out me.

FOWLE. Picked out?

MORGENHALL. Selected.

FOWLE. But I didn't know . . . (*He rises*)

MORGENHALL. No, Mr Fowle. That's the whole beauty of it. You didn't know me. You came to me under a system of chance, invented, like the football pools, to even out the harsh inequality of a world where you have to deserve success. You, Mr Fowle, are my first Dock Brief.

FOWLE. Your Dock . . . ?

MORGENHALL. Brief.

FOWLE. You couldn't explain?

MORGENHALL. Yes, yes, of course.

(*They both cross to* LC)

Criminals with no money and no friends exist. Luckily,
you're one of them. They're entitled to choose any
barrister sitting in court to defend them. The barrister,
however old, gets a brief—(*he moves up* c) and is
remunerated on a modest scale. Busy lawyers, wealthy
lawyers, men with other interests, creep out of court
bent double when the Dock Brief is chosen. (*He moves
down* c) We regulars who are not busy sit on. I've been
a regular for years. It's not etiquette, you see, even if
you want the work, to wave at the prisoner, or whistle,
or try to catch his eye by hoisting any sort of little flag.

FOWLE. Didn't know.

MORGENHALL. But you *can* choose the most advan-
tageous seat. The seat any criminal would naturally
point at. It's the seat under the window, and for ten
years my old friend Tuppy Morgan, bagged it each day
at ten. He sat there, reading *Horace,* and writing to his
innumerable aunts, and almost once a year, a criminal
pointed him out. Oh, Mr Fowle, Tuppy was a limpet
on that seat. But this morning, something, possibly a
cold, perhaps death, kept him indoors. So I had his
place. And you spotted me, no doubt.

FOWLE. Spotted you?

MORGENHALL. My glasses polished. My profile drawn
and learned in front of the great window.

FOWLE. I never noticed.

MORGENHALL. But when they asked you to choose a
lawyer!

FOWLE. I shut my eyes and pointed—I've picked
horses that way, and football teams. Never did me any
good, though, by any stretch of the imagination.

MORGENHALL. So even you, Mr Fowle, didn't choose
me?

FOWLE. Not altogether.

MORGENHALL. The law's a haphazard business.

FOWLE. It does seem chancy.

MORGENHALL. Years of training, and then to be
picked out like a football pool.

FOWLE. Don't take it badly, sir.

MORGENHALL . Of course, you've been fortunate.

FOWLE. So unusual. (*He crosses to the bed*) I was

never one to draw the free bird at Christmas, or guess
the weight of the cake. Now, I'm sorry I told you.

MORGENHALL. Never mind. You hurt me, temporarily, Mr Fowle, I must confess.

(FOWLE *sits on the bed, leans back and puts his
feet up*)

(*He moves the stool to* C) It might have been kinder to
have kept me in ignorance. (*He moves to the table,
picks it up and sets it between the stool and the bed*)
But now it's done. Let's get down to business. And,
Fowle——

FOWLE. Yes, sir?

MORGENHALL. —remember you're dealing with a
fellow man. A man no longer young. Remember the
hopes I've pinned on you and try——

FOWLE. Try . . . ?

MORGENHALL. —try to spare me more pain.

FOWLE. I will, sir. Of course I will.

MORGENHALL (*picking up his brief-case*) Now. (*He
sits on the stool*) Let's get our minds in order. (*He
takes some newspapers, a bottle of medicine, a paper-
backed book and an old envelope from his brief-case,
puts them on the table, then takes a pencil stub from
his pocket, puts the brief-case on the floor and puts on
his spectacles*)

FOWLE. Sort things out.

MORGENHALL. Exactly. Now, this wife of yours.

FOWLE. Doris?

MORGENHALL. Doris. (*He makes notes on the
envelope*) A bitter, unsympathetic woman?

FOWLE. She was always cheerful. She loved jokes.

MORGENHALL. Oh, Fowle. Do be very careful.

FOWLE. I will, sir. But if you'd known Doris . . . She
laughed all day and all night. "Thank God", she'd
say, "for my old English sense of fun."

MORGENHALL. What sort of jokes, Fowle, did this
Doris appreciate?

FOWLE. All sorts.

(MORGENHALL *writes*)

Pictures in the paper. Jokes on the wireless set. Laughs out of crackers, she'd keep them from Christmas to Christmas and trot them out in August.

(MORGENHALL *stops writing and looks up*)

MORGENHALL. You couldn't share it?

FOWLE. Not to that extent. I often missed the funny point.

MORGENHALL. Then you'd quarrel?

FOWLE. "Don't look so miserable, it may never happen." She said that every night when I came home. "Where'd you get that miserable expression from?"

MORGENHALL. I can see it now. There is a kind of Sunday evening appearance to you.

FOWLE. I was quite happy. But it was always, "Cat got your tongue?" "Where's the funeral?" "Play us a tune on that old fiddle face of yours." Then we had to have our tea with the wireless on, so that she'd pick up the phrases.

MORGENHALL. You're not a wireless lover?

FOWLE. I couldn't always laugh. And she'd be doubled up across the table, gasping as if her lungs were full of water. "Laugh," she'd call. "Laugh, damn you. What've you got to be so miserable about?" Then she'd go under, bubbling like a drowning woman.

MORGENHALL (*taking off his spectacles*) Made meals difficult?

FOWLE. Indigestible. I would have laughed, but the jokes never tickled me.

MORGENHALL. They tickled her?

FOWLE. Anything did.

(MORGENHALL *puts on his spectacles and resumes writing*)

Anything a little comic. Our names were misfortunate.

MORGENHALL. Your names?

FOWLE. Fowle. Going down the aisle she said: "Now we're cock and hen, aren't we, old bird?" She laughed so hard we couldn't get her straightened up for the photograph.

MORGENHALL. Fond of puns, I gather you're trying
to say.

FOWLE. Of any sort of joke. I had a little avairy at
the bottom of my garden. As she got funnier so I spent
more time with my birds. Budgerigars are small
parrots. Circles round their eyes give them a sad, tired
look.

MORGENHALL (looking up) You found them sym-
pathetic?

FOWLE. Restful.

(MORGENHALL writes)

Until one of them spoke out at me.

MORGENHALL. Spoke—what words?

FOWLE. "Don't look so miserable, it may never
happen."

MORGENHALL. The bird said that?

FOWLE. She taught it during the day when I was out
at work. It didn't mean to irritate.

MORGENHALL. It was wrong of her, of course. To
lead on your bird like that.

FOWLE (rising and crossing to R) But it wasn't him
that brought me to it. It was Bateson, the lodger.

MORGENHALL (turning in his stool to face Fowle)
Another man?

FOWLE. At long last.

MORGENHALL. I can see it now. A crime of passion.
An unfaithful wife. In flagrante . . . Of course, you
don't know what that means. We'll reduce it to man-
slaughter right away. A wronged husband and there's
never a dry eye in the jury-box. You came in and
caught them.

FOWLE. Always laughing together.

MORGENHALL. Maddening.

FOWLE. He knew more jokes than she did.

MORGENHALL. Stealing her before your eyes?

FOWLE. That's what I thought. He was a big man.
Ex-police. Said he'd been the scream of the station. I
picked him for her specially. In the chitty I put in the
local sweetshop. I wrote: "Humourous type of lodger
wanted."

MORGENHALL. But wasn't that a risk?

FOWLE. Slight, perhaps. But it went all right. Two days after he came he poised a bag of flour to fall on her in the kitchen. Then she sewed up the legs of his pyjamas. They had to hold on to each other so as not to fall over laughing. "Look at old misery standing there," she said, "he can never see anything subtle."

MORGENHALL. Galling for you. Terribly galling.

FOWLE. I thought all was well. (*He moves* C) I spent more time with the birds. I'd come home late and always be careful to scrunch the gravel at the front door. I went to bed early and left them with the Light Programme. On Sunday mornings I fed the budgies and suggested he took her tea in bed. "Laughter," she read out from her horoscope, "leads to love, even for those born under the sign of the virgin."

MORGENHALL. You trusted them. They deceived you.

FOWLE. They deceived me all right. (*He moves to the chair* R *and sits*) And I trusted them to do the right thing. Especially after I'd seen her on his knee and them both looking at the cartoons from one wrapping of chips.

MORGENHALL. Mr Fowle. I'm not quite getting the drift of your evidence. My hope is—your thought may not prove a shade too involved for our literal-minded judge. (*He takes off his spectacles and puts them in the case*) Old Tommy Banter was a rugger blue in ninety-eight. He never rose to chess and his draughts had a brutal unintelligent quality.

FOWLE. When he'd first put his knee under her I thought he'd do the decent thing. I thought I'd have peace in my little house at last. The wireless set dead silent. The end of all that happy laughter. No sound but the twitter from the end of the garden and the squeak of my own foot on the linoleum.

MORGENHALL (*pointing at Fowle with his spectacle case*) You wanted . . .

FOWLE. I heard them whispering together and my hopes raised high. Then I came back and he was gone.

MORGENHALL. She'd . . .

FOWLE. Turned him out. Because he was getting

over familiar. "I couldn't have that," she said. "I may like my laugh, but, thank God, I'm still respectable. No, thank you, there's safety in marriage." She'd sent him away, my last hope.

MORGENHALL. So you . . . ? (*He looks at Fowle and makes a gesture with his spectacle case*)

FOWLE (*nodding*) I realize I did wrong.

MORGENHALL. You could have left.

FOWLE. Who'd have fed the birds? That thought was uppermost.

MORGENHALL. So it's not a crime of passion?

FOWLE. Not if you put it like that.

MORGENHALL (*putting his spectacle case in his pocket*) Mr Fowle. (*He rises*) I've worked and waited for you. (*He moves up* C) Now, you're the only case I've got, *and* the most difficult.

FOWLE. I'm sorry.

MORGENHALL (*moving down* RC) A man could crack his head against a case like you and still be far from a solution. Can't you see how twelve honest hearts will snap like steel when they learn you ended up your wife because she *wouldn't* leave you?

FOWLE. If she had left, there wouldn't have been the need.

MORGENHALL. There's no doubt about it. As I look at you, now, I see you're an unsympathetic figure.

FOWLE. There it is.

MORGENHALL. It'll need a brilliant stroke to save you. (*He moves up* L) An unexpected move—something pulled out of a hat. (*He turns and thumps the table*) I've got it. Something really exciting. The surprise witness.

FOWLE. Witness?

MORGENHALL. Picture the scene, Mr Fowle. The court-room silent. The jury about to sink you. The prosecution flushed with victory. And then I rise, my voice a hoarse whisper, exhausted by that long trial. (*He picks up his wig and puts it on*) "My Lord. If your Lordship pleases."

FOWLE (*rising and moving* C) What are you saying?

MORGENHALL. Good Heavens, man, you don't expect

me do this off the cuff, without any sort of rehearsal?

FOWLE. No . . .

MORGENHALL (*leading Fowle to the table*) Well, come along, man, sit down.

(FOWLE *sits on the table, with his feet on the stool*)

(*He takes the towel from the rail*) Now, this towel over your head, please, to simulate the dirty grey wig. (*He drapes the towel over Fowle's head*) Already you appear anonymous and vaguely alarming. Now, Fowle, forget your personality. You're Sir Tommy Banter, living with a widowed sister in a draughty great morgue on Wimbledon Common. Digestion, bad. Politics, an independent moral Conservative. Diversions, snooker in the basement of the morgue, peeping at the lovers on the Common and money being given away on the television. In love with capital punishment, corporal punishment, and a younger brother who is accomplished at embroidery. A small, alarmed man. Served with distinction in the Great War at sentencing soldiers to long terms of imprisonment. (*He crosses* R *and stands behind the chair*) A man without friends, unexpectedly adored by a great-niece, three years old.

FOWLE. I am?

MORGENHALL. Him.

FOWLE. It feels strange.

MORGENHALL. Now, my Lord. I ask your Lordship's leave to call the surprise witness.

FOWLE. Certainly?

MORGENHALL. What?

FOWLE. Certainly.

MORGENHALL (*crossing to* LC) For Heaven's sake, Fowle, this is like practising bullfights with a kitten. Here's an irregular application by the defence, something that might twist the trial in the prisoner's favour and prevent you catching the connection at Charing Cross. Your breakfast's like a lead weight on your stomach. The dog bit your ankle on the way downstairs. No, blind yourself with rage and terrible justice. (*He crosses to* R *and stands behind the chair*)

FOWLE. No. You can't call the surprise witness.

MORGENHALL. That's better. Oh, my Lord. (*He raises his left arm, facing* L) If your Lordship would listen to me.
FOWLE. Certainly not. You've had your chance. Let's get on with it.
MORGENHALL. My Lord. Justice must not only be done, but must clearly be seen to be done. (*He lowers his arm and faces front*) No-one knows, as yet, what my surprise witness will say. (*He faces* L) Perhaps he'll say the prisoner is guilty in his black heart as your Lordship thinks. (*He faces front*) But perhaps, gentlemen of the jury, we have trapped an innocent. If so, shall we deny him the one door through which he might walk to freedom? The public outcry would never die down.
FOWLE (*snatching off the towel and rising angrily to his feet*) Hear, hear!
MORGENHALL. What's that?
FOWLE. The public outcry.
MORGENHALL. Excellent. Now, towel back on.

(FOWLE *resumes his seat and puts the towel on his head*)

You're the judge.
FOWLE (*as the judge*) Silence! I'll have all those noisy people put out. Very well. Call the witness. But keep it short.
MORGENHALL. Deathly silence as the witness walks through the breathless crowds. Let's see the surprise witness.

(MORGENHALL. *slowly looks from* L *to* R. FOWLE *follows the look.* MORGENHALL *looks at the door.* FOWLE *does the same*)

(*He crosses to Fowle*) Take the towel off.

(FOWLE *rises, moves up* C, *stands on the step and takes off the towel.* MORGENHALL *moves behind the chair*)

FOWLE (*standing very straight*) I swear to tell the truth . . .
MORGENHALL. You've got a real feeling for the Law. A pity you came to it so late in life.

FOWLE. The whole truth . . .
MORGENHALL. Now, what's your name?
FOWLE (*absent-mindedly*) Herbert Fowle.
MORGENHALL (*facing* L *and clapping his hands in annoyance*) The witness.
FOWLE. Martin Jones.
MORGENHALL. Good, good, yes, very good. (*He faces front*) Now, you knew Herbert Fowle?
FOWLE. All my life.
MORGENHALL. Always found him respectable?
FOWLE. Very quiet-spoken man, and clean living.
MORGENHALL. Where was he when this crime took place?
FOWLE. He was . . .
MORGENHALL (*turning to Fowle*) Just a moment. (*He faces* L) My Lord, will you sharpen a pencil and note this down.
FOWLE (*moving* RC) You dare to say that? To him?
MORGENHALL. Fearlessness, Mr Fowle. The first essential in an advocate.

(FOWLE *moves to the table, sits and puts on the towel*)

Is your Lordship's pencil poised?
FOWLE (*as the judge*) Yes, yes. Get on with it.
MORGENHALL. Where was he?

(FOWLE *rises, goes to the step and takes off the towel*)

FOWLE (*as the witness*) In my house.
MORGENHALL. All the evening?
FOWLE. Playing whist. I went to collect him and we left Mrs Fowle well and happy. I returned with him and she'd been removed to the Country and General.
MORGENHALL (*crossing to Fowle*) Panic stirs the prosecution benches. The prosecutor tries a few fumbling questions. But you stand your ground, don't you?
FOWLE. Certainly.
MORGENHALL (*moving behind the chair*) My Lord. I demand the prisoner be released.

(FOWLE *goes to the table, sits and puts on the towel*)

FOWLE (*as the judge*) Certainly. Can't think what all this fuss has been about. Release the prisoner and reduce all police officers in court to the rank of P.C. (*He takes off the towel, rises, goes to the foot of the bed and sits*)

(*There is a pause.* MORGENHALL *takes off his wig and crosses to the table*)

MORGENHALL. Fowle.

FOWLE. Yes, sir?

MORGENHALL. Aren't you going to thank me?

FOWLE. I don't know what I can say.

MORGENHALL. Words don't come easily to you, do they?

FOWLE. Very hard.

MORGENHALL. You could just stand and stammer in a touching way, and offer me that old gold watch of your father's.

FOWLE (*rising*) But . . .

MORGENHALL. Well, I think we've pulled your chestnut out of the fire. We'll just have to make sure of this fellow Jones.

FOWLE (*moving* LC) But . . .

MORGENHALL. Fowle, you're a good chap, but don't interrupt my thinking.

FOWLE. I was only reminding you . . .

MORGENHALL. Well, what?

FOWLE. We have no Jones.

MORGENHALL. Carried off in a cold spell? Then we can get his statement in under the Evidence Act.

FOWLE. He never lived. We made him up.

MORGENHALL (*after a pause*) Fowle. (*He moves* RC)

FOWLE. Yes, sir?

MORGENHALL. It's a remarkable thing—(*he moves* C) but with no legal training, I think you've put your finger on a fatal weakness in our defence.

FOWLE. I was afraid it might be so.

MORGENHALL. It is so.

Fowle (*moving to the downstage end of the bed*)
Then we'd better just give in.

Morgenhall. Give in? (*He crosses to Fowle*) We do
not give in. When my life depends on this case.

Fowle. I forgot. Then we must try.

Morgenhall. Yes. Brain. Brain (*He moves up* c)
Go to work. It'll come to me, you know, in an illumi-
nating flash. Hard, relentless brainwork. This is the
way I go at the crosswords and I never give up. I have
it. (*He moves down* c) Bateson.

Fowle. The lodger?

Morgenhall. Bateson, the lodger. I never liked him.
Under a ruthless cross-examination, you know, he
might confess that it was he. Do you see a flash?

Fowle. You look much happier.

Morgenhall. I am much happier. And when I
begin my ruthless cross-examination . . .

Fowle. Would you care to try it?

Morgenhall. Mr Fowle, you and I are learning to
muck in splendidly together over this. (*He moves
behind the chair and puts on his wig*)

(Fowle *goes on to the doorstep and leans against
the right wall of the doorway-arch, with his hands
in his pockets*)

Mr Bateson.

Fowle (*as Bateson*) Yes, sir?

Morgenhall. Perhaps you'd be good enough to
take your hands out of your pockets when you address
the Court. Not you, Mr Fowle, of course. You became
on very friendly terms with the prisoner's wife?

Fowle. We had one or two good old laughs together.
Ha, ha, ha!

Morgenhall. The association was entirely innocent?

Fowle. Innocent laughs. Jokes without offence. The
cracker or Christmas card variety. No jokes that would
have shamed a postcard.

Morgenhall. And to tell those jokes, did you have
to sit very close to Mrs Fowle?

Fowle. How do you mean?

Morgenhall. Did you have to sit beneath her?

FOWLE. I don't understand.

MORGENHALL. Did she perch upon your knee?

(FOWLE *gives a horrified intake of breath*)

What was that?

FOWLE. Shocked breathing from the jury, sir.

MORGENHALL. Having it's effect, eh? Bateson, will you kindly answer my question.

FOWLE. You're trying to trap me.

MORGENHALL. Not trying Bateson, succeeding.

FOWLE. Well, she may have rested on my knee. Once or twice.

MORGENHALL. And you loved her, guiltily?

FOWLE. I may have done.

MORGENHALL. And planned to take her away with you?

FOWLE. I did ask her.

MORGENHALL. And when she refused . . .

FOWLE. Just a moment. (*He moves to the table, sits and puts on the towel. As the judge*) Where's all this leading?

MORGENHALL. Your Lordship asks me. My Lord, it is our case that it was this man, Bateson, enraged by the refusal of the prisoner's wife to go away with him, who struck . . . (*He crosses to* C) You see where we've go to?

FOWLE (*removing the towel*) I do.

MORGENHALL. Masterly. I think you'll have to agree with me?

FOWLE. Of course.

MORGENHALL. No flaws in this one?

FOWLE. Not really a flaw, sir. Perhaps a little hitch.

MORGENHALL. A hitch. Go on. Break it down.

FOWLE. No, sir, really. (*He rises and moves up* L) Not after you've been so kind.

MORGENHALL. Never mind. All my life I've stood against the winds of criticism and neglect. I am used to hardship. Speak on, Mr Fowle.

FOWLE. Soon as he left my house, Bateson was stopped by an officer. He'd lifted an alarm clock off of me, and the remains of a bottle of port. They booked him in straight away.

MORGENHALL. You mean—(*he faces front*) there wasn't time?

FOWLE. Hardly. Two hours later the next door observed Mrs Fowle at the washing. Then I came home.

MORGENHALL (*turning to Fowle*) Fowle, do you want to help me?

FOWLE. Of course. Haven't I shown it?

MORGENHALL. But you will go on putting all these difficulties in my way.

FOWLE. I knew you'd be upset. (*He sits on the bed*)

MORGENHALL. Not really. After all, I'm a grown-up, even an old man. At my age one expects little gratitude. Oh, I'm not bitter. But a little help, just a very little encouragement . . .

FOWLE. But you'll win this case. A brilliant mind like yours.

MORGENHALL (*moving* RC) Yes. Thank God. It's very brilliant.

FOWLE. And all that training.

MORGENHALL. Years of it. (*He moves to the chair*) Hard, hard training.

FOWLE. You'll solve it, sir.

(*There is a pause.* MORGENHALL *crosses to the up-stage end of the bed, puts a foot up on it and leans over to Fowle*)

MORGENHALL. Fowle. Do you know what I've heard Tuppy Morgan say? After all, he's sat here in court year in, year out, waiting for the Dock Brief himself. "Wilfred," he's frequently told me, "if they ever give you a brief, old fellow, attack the medical evidence. Remember, the jury's full of rheumatism and arthritis and shocking gastric troubles. They love to see a medical man put through it. Always go for a doctor."

FOWLE (*eagerly*) You'd like to try?

MORGENHALL. (*straightening up*) Shall we?

FOWLE. I'd enjoy it. (*He rises and goes on to the step*)

(MORGENHALL *crosses to the chair* R *and leans over the back of it, with one foot on the chair*)

Morgenhall. Doctor, did you say the lady died of heart failure?

Fowle (*as the doctor*) No.

Morgenhall. Come, Doctor, don't fence with me. Her heart wasn't normal when you examined her, was it?

Fowle. She was dead.

Morgenhall. So it had stopped.

Fowle. Yes.

Morgenhall. Then her heart had failed. (*He takes his foot off the chair*)

Fowle. Well . . .

Morgenhall. So she died of heart failure?

Fowle. But . . .

Morgenhall. And heart failure might have been brought on by a fit. I say a fit of laughter at a curiously rich joke on the wireless?

(Fowle *claps his hands, then comes off the step*)

Fowle. Whew!

Morgenhall (*after a pause*) Thank you, Fowle. (*He takes off his wig*) It was kind, but, I thought, hollow. (*He crosses to the stool*) I don't believe my attack on the doctor was convincing. (*He picks up his brief-case, puts it on the table, then sits on the stool*)

Fowle. Perhaps a bit unlikely. But clever.

Morgenhall. Too clever. No. We're not going to win this on science, Fowle. Science must be thrown away. As I asked those questions, I saw I wasn't even convincing you of your own innocence. But you respond to emotion, Fowle, as I do, the magic of oratory, the wonderful power of words.

Fowle. Now you're talking.

Morgenhall. And I shall talk.

Fowle. I wish I could hear some of it. Words as grand as print.

Morgenhall. A golden tongue. A voice like a lyre to charm you out of hell.

Fowle. Now you've commenced to wander away from all I've understood.

Morgenhall. I was drawing on the riches of my

classical education, which comforts me on buses, waiting at surgeries, or in prison cells (*He rises*) But I shall speak to the jury simply, without classical allusions. I shall say . . .

FOWLE. Yes?

MORGENHALL. I shall say . . .

FOWLE. What?

MORGENHALL. I had it on the tip of my tongue.

FOWLE. Oh.

MORGENHALL. I shan't disappoint you. I shall speak for a day, perhaps two days. At the end I shall say . . .

FOWLE. Yes. Just the closing words.

MORGENHALL. The closing words.

FOWLE. To clinch the argument.

MORGENHALL. Yes. The final, irrefutable argument.

FOWLE. If I could only hear.

MORGENHALL. You shall, Fowle. You shall hear it. (*He sits on the stool and takes out his handkerchief*) In court. It'll come out in court, and when I sink back in my seat, exhausted, and wipe the real tears off my glasses . . . (*He replaces his handkerchief in his pocket*)

FOWLE. The judge's summing-up.

MORGENHALL. What will Tommy say?

FOWLE (*as the judge*) Members of the jury . . .

MORGENHALL. Struggling with emotion, as well.

FOWLE. Members of the jury, I can't add anything to the words of the barrister. Go out and consider your verdict.

MORGENHALL. Have they left the box?

FOWLE. Just a formality.

MORGENHALL. I see. I wonder how long they'll be out. (*He pauses*) They're out a long time.

FOWLE. Of course, it must seem long to you. The suspense.

MORGENHALL. I hope they won't disagree.

FOWLE I don't see how they can. Look, they're coming back, sir.

(*There is a pause. FOWLE moves above the table*)

MORGENHALL (*as clerk of the court*) Members of the jury, have you considered your verdict?

FOWLE. We have.

MORGENHALL. And you find the prisoner guilty or not guilty?

FOWLE. Not guilty, my Lord. (*He rushes to the table, sits on it and puts the towel on his head*)

MORGENHALL (*rising and waving his wig*) Hooray!

FOWLE (*as the judge*) Now, if there's any sort of Mafeking around, I'll have the court closed.

MORGENHALL. So I'm surrounded, mobbed. Tuppy Morgan wrings my hand and says it was lucky he left the seat. The judge sends me a letter of congratulation. The journalist dart off to their little telephones. And what now? "Of course, they'd make you a judge but you're probably too busy . . ." There's a queue of solicitors on the stairs. My old clerk writes on my next brief, "A thousand guineas to divorce a duchess". There are questions of new clothes, laying down the port. Oh, Mr Fowle, the change in life you've brought me.

FOWLE (*rising*) It will be your greatest day. (*He removes the towel and crosses to* C)

MORGENHALL. Yes, Mr Fowle. (*He crosses to Fowle*) My greatest day.

(*The bolts shoot back and the door slowly opens*)

(*He moves up* C) What's that? I said we weren't to be interrupted. It's draughty in here with that door open. (*He calls*) Close it, there's a good chap, do. (*He moves down* C *to* L *of Fowle*)

FOWLE. I think, you know, they must want us for the trial. (*He moves up* RC, *takes his jacket off the peg, goes to the chair, and sits and puts on his jacket*)

MORGENHALL *puts on his wig, puts the papers, medicine bottle, etc. in his brief-case, leaves the brief-case on the table, moves to the bed, picks up his gown and struggles to put it on.* FOWLE *rises, crosses to Morgenhall and assists him.* MORGENHALL *goes to the door, remembers his brief-case, returns and picks it up.* FOWLE *does a "thumbs-up" sign.* MORGENHALL *nods, and with a dramatic sweep of his gown, exits.* Fowle *follows him off, and the lights dim to* Black-Out *as—*

the Curtain *falls*

SCENE II

Scene—*The same.*

When the Curtain *rises, the sky through the window shows that it is late afternoon. The table has been replaced under the window and the stool is* lc. *The cell is empty. The door opens.* Morgenhall *enters. He is without his wig and gown and is more agitated than ever. He stands by the open door and speaks to an unseen warder off.*

Morgenhall. He's not here at the moment—he's not . . . ? Oh, I'm glad. Just out temporarily? With the Governor? Then, I'll wait for him. Poor soul. How's he taking it? Well, I'll just sit down here and wait for Mr Fowle.

(*The door closes*)

(*He whistles for a few moments*) "May it please you, my Lord—*members* of the jury . . ." I should have said, "May it please you, my *Lord*—members of the jury . . ." (*He moves to the stool and sits*) I should have said—"Members of the jury. Is there one of you who doesn't crave for peace—crave for peace. The silence of an undisturbed life, the dignity of an existence without dependants—without jokes. Have you never been tempted? I should have said, "Members of the *jury*. You and I are men of the world . . ." "If your Lordship would kindly not interrupt my speech to the jury." "I'm obliged." "Members of the jury, before I was so rudely interrupted . . ." I might have said, "Look at the prisoner, members of the jury. Has he hurt you, done you the slightest harm? Is he not the mildest of men? He merely took it upon himself to regulate his domestic affairs. An Englishman's home is his castle. Do any of you feel a primitive urge, members of the jury, to be revenged on this gentle bird-fancier? Members of the jury, I see I'm affecting your emotions, but let us consider the weight of the evidence." Might have said that. (*He rises and paces* L *and* R) I might have said—(*with distress*) I might have said something . . .

> (*The door opens.*
> FOWLE *enters. He is smiling to himself, but as soon as he sees Morgenhall he looks serious and solicitous. The door closes*)

FOWLE. I was hoping you'd find time to drop in, sir. I'm afraid you're upset.

MORGENHALL. No, no, my dear chap. (*He moves down* L) Not at all upset.

FOWLE. The result of the trial's upset you.

MORGENHALL. I feel a little dashed. A little out of sorts.

FOWLE. It was disappointing for you.

MORGENHALL. A touch of disappointment. But there'll be other cases. There may be other cases.

FOWLE. But you'd built such high hopes on this particular one.

MORGENHALL. Well, there it is, Fowle. (*He moves to the stool and sits*)

FOWLE. It doesn't do to expect too much of a particular thing.

MORGENHALL. You're right, of course.

FOWLE (*crossing below Morgenhall to the bed*) Year after year, I used to look forward keenly to the Feathered Friends Fanciers' annual do. (*He sits on the downstage end of the bed*) Invariably it took the form of a dinner.

MORGENHALL. Your yearly treat?

FOWLE. Exactly. All I had in the enjoyment line. Each year I built high hopes on it. "June thirteenth," I'd say, "now there's an evening to look forward to."

MORGENHALL. Something to live for?

FOWLE. In a way. But when it came, you know, it was never up to it. Your collar was always too tight, or the food was inadequate, or someone had a nasty scene with the fancier in the chair. So, on June fourteenth, I always said to myself: "Thank God for a night at home."

MORGENHALL. It came and went and your life didn't change?

FOWLE. No, quite frankly.

MORGENHALL. And this case has left me just as I was before.

FOWLE. Don't say that.

MORGENHALL. Tuppy Morgan's back in his old seat under the window. The judge never congratulated me. No-one's rung up to offer me a brief. I thought my old clerk looked coldly at me, and there was a titter in the luncheon-room when I ordered my usual roll and tomato soup.

FOWLE. But, I . . .

MORGENHALL (*rising and moving up* R) And you're not left in a very favourable position.

FOWLE. Well, it's not so bad for me. After all, I had no education.

MORGENHALL (*turning to face Fowle*) So many years before I could master the Roman Law relating to the ownership of chariots . . .

FOWLE. Wasted, you think?

MORGENHALL. I feel so.

FOWLE. But without that rich background, would an individual have been able to sway the Court as you did?

MORGENHALL. Sway?

FOWLE. The Court?

MORGENHALL. Did I do that?

FOWLE. It struck me you did.

MORGENHALL. Indeed . . .

FOWLE. It's turned out masterly.

MORGENHALL. Mr Fowle, you're trying to be kind. (*He moves down* LC) When I was a child, I played French cricket with an uncle who deliberately allowed the ball to strike his legs. At the age of seven that irked me. At my age I can face the difficulties of accurate batting . . .

FOWLE. But, no, sir. (*He rises and moves to* L *of Morgenhall*) I owe it all to you. Where I am.

MORGENHALL. I'm afraid near the end.

FOWLE. Just commencing.

MORGENHALL. I lost, Mr Fowle. You may not be aware of it. It may not have been hammered home to you, yet. (*He crosses below Fowle to the bed*) But your case is lost. (*He sits on the downstage end of the bed*)

FOWLE. But there are ways and ways of losing.

MORGENHALL. That's true, of course.

FOWLE (*moving to the bed and sitting beside Morgenhall*) I noticed your artfulness right at the start, when the policeman gave evidence. You pulled out that red handkerchief, slowly and deliberately, like a conjuring trick.

MORGENHALL. And blew?

FOWLE. A sad, terrible trumpet.

MORGENHALL. Unnerved him, I thought.

FOWLE. He never recovered. There was no call to ask questions after that.

MORGENHALL. And then they called that doctor.

FOWLE. You were right not to bother with him.

MORGENHALL. Tactics, you see. We'd decided not to trouble with science.

FOWLE. So we had. And with Bateson . . .

MORGENHALL. No, Fowle. I must beware of your flattery. I think I might have asked Bateson . . .

FOWLE. It wouldn't have made a farthing's difference. A glance told them he was a demon.

MORGENHALL. He stood there, so big and red, with his no tie and dirty collar. I rose up to question him and suddenly it seemed as if there were no reason for us to converse. I remembered what you said about his jokes, his familiarity with your wife. I turned from him in disgust. I think that jury guessed the reason for my silence with friend Bateson.

FOWLE. I think they did.

MORGENHALL. But when it came to the speech . . .

FOWLE. The best stroke of all.

MORGENHALL. I can't agree. You no longer carry me with you.

FOWLE. Said from the heart.

MORGENHALL. I'm sure of it. But not, dare I say, altogether justified. We can't pretend, can we, Mr Fowle, that the speech was a success?

FOWLES. It won the day.

MORGENHALL. I beg you not to be under any illusions. They found you guilty.

FOWLE. But that masterly speech . . .

MORGENHALL. I can't be hoodwinked.

FOWLE (rising) I stood up, Mr Fowle, and it was the moment I'd waited for. Ambition had driven me to it, the moment when I was alone with what I wanted. Everyone turned to me, twelve blank faces in the jury box, eager to have the grumpy looks wiped off them. The judge was silent. The prosecutor courteously pretended to be asleep. I only had to open my mouth and pour words out. What stopped me?

FOWLE. What?

MORGENHALL. Fear. That's what's suggested. That's what the clerks tittered to the waitresses in the luncheon-room. Old Wilf Morgenhall was in a funk.

FOWLE. More shame on them.

MORGENHALL. But it wasn't so. (He crosses to c) Nor did my mind go blank. When I stood up I knew exactly what I was going to say.

FOWLE. Then, why . . . ?

MORGENHALL. "Not say it"—you were going to ask?

FOWLE (turning to face Morgenhall) It had struck me . . .

MORGENHALL. It must have, Fowle. It must have struck many people. (He moves up c) You'll forgive a reminiscence?

FOWLE (sitting on the downstage end of the bed) Glad of one.

MORGENHALL. The lady I happened to mention yesterday. I don't, of course, often speak of her . . .

FOWLE. She, who, in the nineteen-fourteen . . . ?

MORGENHALL. Exactly. But I lost her long before that. For years, you know, Mr Fowle, this particular

lady and I met at tea-parties, tennis, and so on. Then,
one evening, I walked home with her. We stood on
Vauxhall Bridge. It was a warm summer night, and
silence fell. It was the moment when I should have
spoken, the obvious moment. Then, something over-
came me, it wasn't shyness or fear, then, but a
tremendous exhaustion. I was tired out by the long
wait, and when the opportunity came—all I could
think of was sleep.

FOWLE. It's a relief . . .

MORGENHALL. To go home alone. To undress, clean
your teeth, knock out your pipe, not to bother with
failure or success.

FOWLE. So yesterday . . .

MORGENHALL. I had lived through that moment so
many times. It happened every day in my mind, day-
dreaming on buses, or in the doctor's surgery. When it
came, I was tired of it. The exhaustion came over me.
I wanted it to be all over. I wanted to be alone in my
room, in the darkness, with a soft pillow round my
ears. So I failed.

FOWLE. Don't say that, sir.

MORGENHALL. Being too tired to make my day-
dream public. (*He moves up* RC) It's a nice day. (*He
moves* R *and glances at the window*) Summer's coming.
(*He faces front*) I think I shall retire from the Bar.

FOWLE. Don't say it, sir. After that rigorous training.

MORGENHALL. Well, there it is. I think I shall retire.

FOWLE. But, cheer up, sir. (*He rises and moves* C) As
you said, other cases, other days. Let's take this calmly,
sir. (*He crosses to Morgenhall and seats him on the
chair*) Let's be very lucid, as you put it in your own
statement.

MORGENHALL. Other cases? I'm getting on, you
know. Tuppy Morgan's back in his place. I doubt if
the Dock Brief will come round again.

FOWLE. But there'll be something.

MORGENHALL. What can there be? Unless . . . ?

FOWLE. Yes, sir?

MORGENHALL. There would be another brief if . . .

FOWLE. Yes?

MORGENHALL. I advised you to appeal.

FOWLE. Ah, now that, misfortunately . . . (*He turns away* L)

MORGENHALL (*rising*) There's a different atmosphere there, up in the Appeal Court, Fowle. It's far from the rough and tumble, question and answer—(*he crosses down* L) swear on the Bible and lie your way out of it. It's quiet up there, pure law, of course. Yes. I believe I'm cut out for the Court of Appeal. (*He moves up* C)

FOWLE. But, you see. . .

MORGENHALL. A big, quiet Court in the early summer afternoon. Piles of books, and when you put one down the dust and powdered leather rises and makes the ushers sneeze. The clock ticks. Three old judges in scarlet take snuff with trembling hands. You'll sit in the dock and not follow a legal word. And I'll give them all my Law and get you off on a technicality.

FOWLE. But, today . . .

MORGENHALL. Now, if I may remind your Lordships of Prickle against the Haverfordwest Justices *ex parte* Anger, reported in ninety-six *Moor's Ecclesiastical* at page a thousand and three.

(FOWLE *sits on the chair*)

Have your Lordships the report? Lord Bradwell, C.J., says, at the foot of the page, "The guilty intention is a deep foundation-stone in the wall of our jurisprudence. So if it be that Prickle did run the bailiff through with his *poignard* taking him for a stray dog or cat, it seems there would be well raised the plea of *autrefois* mistake. But contra if he thought him to be his neighbour's cat, then, as my Brother Broadwinkle has well said in Lord Roche and Anderson, there might fall out a constructive larceny and *felo in rem*." (*He moves to Fowle*) Oh, Mr Fowle, I have some of these fine cases by heart.

FOWLE. Above me, I'm afraid, you're going now.

MORGENHALL. Of course I am. These cases always bore the prisoner until they're upheld or overruled and he comes out dead or alive at the end of it all. Thank God, I kept my books. I shall open them up and say— I shall say . . .

FOWLE (*rising and crossing to* LC) It's no good.

MORGENHALL. What's no good?

FOWLE. It's no good appealing.

MORGENHALL. No good?

FOWLE (*sitting on the stool*) No good at all.

MORGENHALL (*moving down* C) Mr Fowle. I've worked hard for you.

FOWLE. That's true, sir.

MORGENHALL. And I mean to go on working.

FOWLE. It's a great comfort . . .

MORGENHALL. In the course of our close, and may I say it—yes, our happy collaboration on this little crime of yours, I've become almost fond of you.

FOWLE. Thank you, sir, but I . . .

MORGENHALL. At first, I have to admit it, I was put off by your somewhat furtive and repulsive appearance. I saw in you a man marked by all the physical signs of confirmed criminality.

FOWLE. No oil painting?

MORGENHALL. Let's agree on that at once.

FOWLE. The wife thought so, too.

MORGENHALL. Enough of her, poor woman.

FOWLE. Oh, agreed.

MORGENHALL. My first solicitude for your well-being, let's face this, as well, had a selfish element. You were my very own case, and I didn't want to lose you.

FOWLE. Natural feelings. But still . . .

MORGENHALL. I haven't wounded you?

FOWLE. Nothing fatal, sir.

MORGENHALL. I'm glad. Because, you know, as we worked on this case, together, an affection sprang up . . .

FOWLE. Mutual.

MORGENHALL. You seemed to have a real desire to help, and, if I may say so, an instinctive taste for the law.

FOWLE. A man can't go through this sort of thing without getting legal interests.

MORGENHALL. Quite so. But I did notice, just at the start, some flaws in you as a client.

FOWLE. Flaws?

MORGENHALL. You may not care to admit it. But
let's, be honest. After all, we don't want to look on the
dreary side! but you may be with us for very long . . .
    FOWLE (*rising*) That's what I was trying to say . . .
    MORGENHALL. Please, Mr Fowle, don't interrupt, not
until we've—

(FOWLE *sits on the stool*)

—cleared this out of the way. Now, didn't you, just at
the beginning, put unnecessary difficulties before us?
    FOWLE. Did I?
    MORGENHALL. I well remember, before I got a bit of
keenness into you, that you seemed about to admit
your guilt.
    FOWLE. Oh . . .
    MORGENHALL. Just a little obstinate, wasn't it?
    FOWLE. I dare say . . .
    MORGENHALL. And now, when I've worked for fifty
years to get the law at my fingertips, I hear you mutter,
"No appeal".
    FOWLE (*turning to Morgenhall*) No appeal!
    MORGENHALL. Mr Fowle . . .
    FOWLE (*rising*) Yesterday, you asked me to spare you
pain, sir. This is going to be very hard for me.
    MORGENHALL. What?
    FOWLE (*moving* R) As you say, we've worked to-
gether, and I've had the pleasure of watching the tick-
ing over of a legal mind. If you'd call any afternoon I'd
be pleased to repay the compliment by showing you my
birds.
    MORGENHALL. Not in this world, you must realize,
unless we appeal.
    FOWLE. You see—this morning I saw the governor.
    MORGENHALL. You had some complaint?
    FOWLE. I don't want to boast, but the truth is—he
sent for me.
    MORGENHALL. You went in fear . . .
    FOWLE. And trembling.
    MORGENHALL. And trembling.
    FOWLE (*moving up* R) But he turned out a very
gentlemanly sort of individual. Ex-army, I should

imagine. All the ornaments of a gentleman. (*He moves down* C) Wife and children in a tinted photo framed on the desk, handsome oil painting of a prize pig over the mantelpiece. Healthy red face. Strong smell of scented soap . . .

MORGENHALL (*sitting on the stool*) But grow to the point . . .

FOWLE. I'm telling you. "Well, Fowle," he says. "Sit down, do. I'm just finishing this letter." (*He sits on the chair*) So I sat and looked out of his windows. Big wide windows in the governor's office, and the view . . .

MORGENHALL. Fowle. If this anecdote has any point, be a good chap—reach it.

FOWLE. Of course it has— where was I?

MORGENHALL. Admiring the view.

FOWLE. Panoramic, it was. Well, this governor individual, finishing his letter, lit up one of those flat type of Egyptian cigarettes. "Well, Fowle," he said . . .

MORGENHALL. Yes, yes. It's not necessary, Fowle, to reproduce every word of this conversation. Give us the gist, just the meat, you understand. Leave out the trimmings.

FOWLE. Trimmings there weren't. He put it quite bluntly.

MORGENHALL. What did he put?

FOWLE. "Well, Fowle, this may surprise you." (*He rises and crosses to Morgenhall*) "But the Home Office was on the phone about you this morning, and . . ." Isn't that a government department?

MORGENHALL. Yes, yes. And well . . . ?

FOWLE. It seems they do, in his words, come through from time to time, and just on business, of course, on that blower. And quite frankly, he admitted he was as shocked as I was. But the drill is, as he phrased it, a reprieve.

MORGENHALL. A . . . ?

FOWLE. It's all over. I'm free.

MORGENHALL. Free?

FOWLE. It seems that trial was no good at all.

MORGENHALL. No good. But why?

FOWLE (*crossing to* R) Oh, no particular reason.

Morgenhall (*rising and crossing to Fowle*) There
must be a reason. Nothing happens in the law without
a reason.
Fowle. You won't care to know.
Morgenhall. Tell me.
Fowle. You're too busy to wait.
Morgenhall. Tell me, Mr Fowle, why this governor,
who knows nothing of the law; should have called our
one and only trial together "no good".
Fowle. You yourself taught me not to scatter in-
formation like bombs.
Morgenhall. Mr Fowle, you must answer my question. My legal career may depend on it. If I'm not to
have wasted my life on useless trials.
Fowle. You want to hear?
Morgenhall. Certainly.
Fowle. He may not have been serious. (*He moves
above the chair*) There was a twinkle, most likely, in
his eye.
Morgenhall. But he said . . .
Fowle. That the barrister they chose for me was no
good. "An old crock," in his words. No good at all.
That he never said a word in my defence. So my case
never got to the jury. He said the whole business was
ever so null and void, but I'd better be careful in the
future. (*He moves to Morgenhall*) Don't you see? If I'd
had a barrister who asked questions and made clever
speeches I'd be as dead as mutton. Your artfulness
saved me.
Morgenhall. My . . .
Fowle. The artful way you handled it. The dumb
tactics. They paid off! I'm alive!
Morgenhall. There is that . . .
Fowle. And so are you.
Morgenhall. We both are . . . ?
Fowle. I'm free.
Morgenhall. To go back to your birds. (*He moves
up LC, then returns to L of Fowle*) I suppose . . .
Fowle. Yes, Mr Morgenhall?
Morgenhall. It's unlikely you'll marry again?
Fowle. Unlikely.

(There is a pause. Morgenhall *crosses above Fowle to the chair and moves it down* R)

Morgenhall. But you have the clear appearance of a criminal. I suppose it's not impossible, that you might commit some rather more trivial offence.

Fowle. A man can't live, Mr Morgenhall, without committing some trivial offences. Almost daily.

Morgenhall. Then we may meet again. You may need my services . . .

Fowle. Constantly.

Morgenhall. The future may not be so black . . .

Fowle. The sun's shining.

*(*Morgenhall *turns to the window, then turns again to Fowle)*

Morgenhall. Can we go?

Fowle *(moving to the door)* I think the door's been open some time.

*(*Morgenhall *follows Fowle to the door.* Fowle *tries the door. It is unbolted and swings open)*

After you, Mr Morgenhall, please.

Morgenhall. No, no.

Fowle. A man of your education should go first.

Morgenhall. I think you should lead the way, Mr Fowle, and as your legal adviser I will follow, at a discreet distance, to iron out such little angles as you may hope to leave in your wake. Let's go.

Morgenhall *whistles his fragment of tune.* Fowle *joins in. Whistling, they leave the cell.* Morgenhall *executing, as he leaves, the steps of a small, delighted dance.*

Slow Curtain

FURNITURE AND PROPERTY LIST

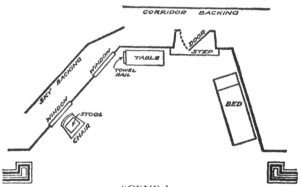

SCENE I

On stage: Bed. *On it:* pillow, 2 dark blankets
Table. *On it:* Bible
    Under it: enamel bucket
Towel rail. *On it:* towel. Chair, Stool
    On hook on wall: Fowle's jacket
Off stage: Brief-case. *In it:* newspapers, bottle of medicine,
    paper-backed book, old envelope (MORGEN-
    HALL.)
Personal: MORGENHALL.: legal wig, spectacles in case, pencil
    stub, handkerchief

SCENE II

Setting as Scene I
Replace table up R

LIGHTING PLOT

Property fittings required: none
    Interior. A prison cell. The same scene throughout
    THE APPARENT SOURCE OF LIGHT is a window R
    THE MAIN ACTING AREAS are RC, C and LC
SCENE I
To open: Effect of sunshine
Cue 1   At the end of the Scene   (Page 24)
    Dim all lights to BLACK-OUT
SCENE II
To open: Effect of late afternoon sunshine. *No cues*

Lightning Source UK Ltd.
Milton Keynes UK
UKOW06f0952100116

266087UK00001B/12/P